THE ART OF SaaS

THE ART OF SAAS

*A Primer on the Fundamentals of
Building and Running a Healthy
SaaS Business*

Ahmed Bouzid

David Rennyson

Library of Congress Control Number: 2015900536
ISBN: Hardcover   978-1-5035-3452-0
                Softcover   978-1-5035-3453-7
                eBook   978-1-5035-3454-4

Rev. date: 01/20/2015

To order additional copies of this book, contact:
Xlibris
1-888-795-4274
www.Xlibris.com
Orders@Xlibris.com
701456

CONTENTS

SaaS

In SaaS circles, suggesting that a vendor's architecture is anything less than fully multi-tenant is tantamount to questioning a man's virility or impugning an American's patriotism.

—Phil Wainewright

SaaS is a way of *being*. It is a way of life, a world conception, a paradigm, and an ecosystem.

Some even say that SaaS is a *religion*.

SaaS is not another software delivery configuration or a set of features in a continuum of alternatives.

SaaS is a *business model* that requires interlocking functions that combine to enable the delivery of *the SaaS promise*.

THE SaaS PROMISE

The SaaS promise is the bold proposition made by the vendor to their customers that the vendor will deliver *(1) highly reliable access to (2) highly usable software through a simple web browser, available from (3) anywhere at (4) anytime.*

Customers buy SaaS for many reasons. They buy because (1) they do not want to manage hardware; (2) they do not want to manage software; (3) they do not want to spend money up front; (4) they want to iteratively deploy; (5) their business is scaling up or down; (6) they have been frustrated by long deployment intervals of on-premise systems; (7) they have been frustrated by nonresponsive "hosted" software providers; (8) they don't want to pay for features they don't use; (9) they want to moderate their investment as a monthly spend; (10) they do not want to invest in technologies or methodologies that may be obsolete in less than three years.

Above all, SaaS customers want to minimize risk for themselves and transfer risk to their vendors.

SaaS Fundamentals

True SaaS delivers *one software stack* attached to *one database schema* to *one customer install base*.

True SaaS is *Multitenant*.

True SaaS delivers its software service over the Internet. A simple litmus test as to whether or not a provider is a SaaS provider is the availability of a login from the home page to the core service. From that login, one should be able to immediately sign up and begin consuming the offering.

In true SaaS, the billing begins immediately upon sign-up. A SaaS scheduling system should be able to grid its first schedule within hours. It should be intuitive and *lead* the designer (who is not a programmer) through the logical steps to instantiate an application in its relevant domain.

True SaaS doesn't require its customers to download software—*ever!*

True SaaS is as different from hosted SaaS as hosted SaaS is different from on-premise software.

True SaaS is actually closer to on-premise software than to hosted SaaS.

In true SaaS, the customer is empowered to conceive, design, deploy, and use the services as if they owned and deployed the software on their own premise.

In hosted SaaS, by contrast, the customer is effectively hostage to vendor staff and chained to the chosen technology framework.

True SaaS is about *control without the overhead of control.*

An on-premise install gives the customer total control, but at the cost of up-front hardware, up-front licenses, and an expensive staff to run the install and maintain the separate instance over time.

Hosted SaaS unloads the delivery headaches, but at the expense of control: the hosted, managed service is now mediated by an external staff that may or may not be responsive and, when responsive, may leverage its position of power.

In true SaaS, *the customer can serve themselves directly.*

True SaaS is *liberating.*

True SaaS requires *an immense degree of trust* by the customer of the vendor. The customer is trusting the vendor with *their very business.*

By the same token, true SaaS requires *an immense degree of competence* on the part of the vendor. Delivering the SaaS promise is not trivial. Successfully delivering the SaaS promise is wound up from hundreds of diligent iterative improvements.

True SaaS involves putting security, uptime, and client success at the heart of product development. This involves training, process, discipline, standards, and customers.

As a result, true SaaS is nearly impossible to get started from any other state than from scratch. Deploying successful true on-demand SaaS requires the adoption of a highly user-centric philosophy that makes the usability, security, and performance of the software and the service at the core of the offering.

True SaaS observes the user and how they interact with the software and iteratively adapts to them as it grows, with an eye to converging toward a healthy, market-sustainable, profitable product—in SaaS, the concept of minimum viable product morphs into that of the minimum sustainable product.

The SaaS Bargain

In exchange for transferring all risk to the vendor, the customer must assume the responsibility for using the software as it is offered. It is the buyers' responsibility to decide whether the SaaS offering is good enough for their business needs. If it is not a good fit, the customer should continue shopping, partner with the closest product, and collaborate as the road map evolves, buy on-premise software, or hire a consultant to build the software from scratch.

It is an **ethical failure** for the buyer to purchase SaaS and then immediately begin making demands that the vendor mangle and deform their product for the sake of satisfying the buyer's specific needs. Such demands strike at the very heart of the SaaS bargain:

> I, the vendor, will assume the risk of building and hosting a piece of software for a large customer base, but in exchange, my buyers will use the software and the service that I am offering them as is.

A corollary of this axiom is for the vendor not to sell under false pretense: not to pretend that they have features that they may not have or to knowingly remain silent on significant issues that will inevitably emerge after closing the deal or to promise features that may not be on the product road map or that may not be delivered on time.

SaaS Service Operations

True SaaS is not for the fainthearted.

In true SaaS, *the platform is part of the product*. It is a feature of the product. It does not live separately from the product.

Therefore, when the platform is not available, the product itself is not available.

Anything less than 100 percent uptime breaks the promise of SaaS.

Customers are not forgiving on uptime because they believe that they can do better—even if they have never operated a platform above 99.9 percent uptime.

An unplanned service outage potentially affects *all customers*, and it affects all customers *at the same time*. In what other business model can you take out all customers at once?

In the case of enterprise SaaS serving mission-critical operations, such as a contact center or service desk, the downtime can be deadly: customers will leave if they feel that their business is being placed at risk by using your services. In many cases, they will depart months after an outage and without notification or warning.

Unplanned disruptions cause a myriad of ill effects:

1. they cause an avalanche of support activity that will overwhelm your teams—emotionally and physically;
2. they upset the sales activities of your farmers, who will be suddenly deputized by the support team;
3. cross-sell cycles will either be lengthened or cancelled;
4. hunter sales cycles themselves may be upset if demos do not work or a prospect hears about the downtime from a customer or a reference;
5. engineering resources may need to be diverted to produce a patch, which would then need to be certified by a quality-assurance team that may have been certifying a new build, and
6. the road map will see delays in new product features, further affecting customers.

Crucial to the SaaS operation is *timely communication*: if and when a disruption occurs, the SaaS provider gains immense customer good will by (1) communicating immediately upon disruption, (2) keeping customers informed while the disruption is being resolved, and (3) appraising the customers with a postmortem, explaining: (a) why the disruption happened, (b) what was done to remedy it, and (c) what has been done or will be done to prevent its occurrence in the future.

The best cure to the ills described above is striving for the Holy Grail of *100 percent uptime*.

Managing SaaS Uptime

One hundred percent uptime is achievable.

The following are the fourteen constructs of high-performance SaaS operations. An entire book could be written on each of these bullets. But together they form a solid checklist for examining a SaaS operations and engineering team.

1. **Establish and maintain well-defined procedures**: Ensure the entire product life cycle is written down, trained upon, and followed, including development life cycle, change management, incident management, and problem management.

2. **Actively manage security compliance**: This includes a continual review of security standards, third-party review and third-party auditing and testing.

3. **Establish well-defined action plans**: This requires documentation of all error messages that can be produced, what they mean, and actions to take when they occur.

4. **Establish hardened standard-operation procedures (SOPs)**: This helps with on-boarding of new hires and with the introduction of new software or services. Within days or weeks, new team members should know the steps of escalation, the steps of reaction, and when and how to fail

over pods and sites. If they are not that simple, your response time in real time with even your best employees will be too slow to avoid prolonged interruption of service.

5. **Ensure platform segmentation/clustering**: Ability to segment the platform to route around issues and define a "known" quantity of hardened performance units (example, a full stack that can handle one thousand concurrent users—better to have ten of these than one thousand-unit stack).

6. **Engineer and plan for high availability**: Design solutions that are fault tolerant (highly available) to include georedundancy, "pod" redundancy, and component redundancy.

7. **Ensure platform visibility**: Both from a physical perspective as well as an application or software perspective. Use tools that look at each layer of the stack from physical connectivity to application layer database input output layer.

8. **Ensure constant monitoring and alerting**: The ability to be notified as errors occur must be highly structured, automated, and organized. Tools should be deployed at all levels of the application stack.

9. **Establish and manage daily change control**: Ensure that change actions, no matter how small, are communicated, exposing dependencies and socializing the risk potential. Almost all outages are caused by recent changes in the infrastructure or software.

10. **Ensure collaboration and communication**: Continual communication and collaboration across the support, operations, engineering, and product organizations. Build strong teamwork across these functions.

11. **Conduct thorough root-cause analysis reviews**: Continual review of incidents to understand what needs to improve (process, visibility, architecture, software).

12. **Test thoroughly**: Every new software release should be run through a highly automated regression test of a known unit. This known unit should have a defined number of users, a traffic volume target, and the concurrency level the platform can handle. It can be a complete rack of a working solution with a single instance of software and related components attached. This unit should we call a "pod." Each pod should be tested with every new release and point release at varying degrees of load and traffic complexity and certified at a known capacity level by your quality-assurance (QA) team. If you know your new software can perform in a pod equally in your benchmark tests at full load before you deploy, you minimize risk.

13. **Phase releases**: Roll releases across pods so you can siphon traffic on and off the new software and minimize risk to individual traffic out of hours.

14. **Manage capacity:** Really. A monthly meeting of thirty minutes to review capacity forecasts, utilization, peaks, and areas of bottleneck at the component and platform level can signal emerging capacity issues months in advance.

SaaS Development

Software built for SaaS is software built to run on **one common infrastructure** and delivered to **one set of customers**. It does not need every feature at once to be successful. It must be designed for **multitenancy, high availability, high security,** and **high usability**. This is the minimum sustainable product. Once this state is achieved, the development team can operate at increasing levels of capacity and feature complexity.

Such software needs to be built for:

1. **Performance**: It must be fast, highly available, and free of bugs, given that the cost of a bug or outage is often the loss of customers (see "SaaS Service Operations" above).

2. **Scalability**: The provider has no control over when or how a stress on the service will occur. The service needs to be scalable horizontally (a spike in the number of simultaneous users) and vertically (a spike in the use of a particular feature or subset of features (see "Capacity Planning in Uptime" above).

3. **Configurability**: A layer of control that will enable turning features on or off is fundamental to the delivery and the selling of one software to all. It is the mechanism through which added value can be offered at a premium while remaining

true to the one-install-for-all model. In SaaS, features should be enabled and disabled, not installed.

4. **Data integrity**: In true SaaS, all customers share the same *one database schema*. This raises red flags in the mind of the customer: What if the software makes a mistake and now my data is being viewed by another customer? Data must be segregated to the degree that is necessary for your business segment, but without jeopardizing the one-install-for-all architecture.

5. **Privacy and security**: Similar to integrity—how can the customer be assured that shared data will be protected? One solitary instance of private data leaking may cause mass defection of customers and significant corporate liability.

6. **Integration:** To prosper, a SaaS cloud needs to be able to connect to other SaaS clouds. It needs to have its cloud exposed to other clouds with an API offering, and it needs to be able to connect to other clouds via their respective API offerings. Such integration must be made easy to enable the proliferation of value-added solutions and the emergence of a healthy and thriving cloud ecosystem.

SaaS Security

The specter of security is so great that SaaS providers must undertake a security program unlike traditional enterprise software providers.

The SaaS provider must secure: (1) the data center, (2) the data, and (3) the processes surrounding deployments and customer interactions. These must be secured to a level of quality that is at least as good as the level that the customer can achieve (or thinks they can achieve) independently. This means the higher the caliber of customers, the higher the standard of record.

Most SaaS platform security programs can be delivered through a three-part program including

1. **SSAE 16**: Surrounding the data center. This can be achieved by finding a data center provider that will attest to this standard in the early days. There is no need to deploy a standalone data center; simply find one that can support this standard for you.

2. **PCI Compliance**: Payment-card-industry-compliance standards are the most specific, well-documented, and practical standards available. If PCI compliance can be achieved, such compliance can act as a proxy for many other forms of personally identifiable information (PII). Chief information security officers at large enterprise firms understand and respect this standard. Further, PCI compliance

can be certified by a third party who conducts annual audits along with robust training. This moves your sales and operations team from a "claim" to a "seal of approval."

3. **Industry and international process standards**: For certain industries, this is critical and can range from Gramm-Leach-Bliley (finance and insurance) to Health Insurance Portability and Accountability Act (HIPAA) (healthcare). Once PCI is in place, incrementally adding industry-specific tests to the program based on sales cycles in relevant industries, this will enable you to satisfy the concerns of large customers who are required to comply with such regulation. In some areas of the world, ISO 27001 is one such standard that gives comfort to enterprises. Unfortunately, none of these standards have the "specifics" or universal rigor and acceptance of PCI-DSS. This means lots of room for interpretation, rework, and second-guessing by various auditors. Choose these additional standards (and industries) carefully based on your budget and commercial aspirations.

SaaS Testing

Because all customers are running on the same software stack, a bug or a defect that slips through quality-assurance cracks can cause a significant cascade of disruptions that affect the whole business ecosystem (see "Service Operations").

When certifying for SaaS deployments, the quality-assurance team is certifying two things: the *integrity of the continually running base* and *the delta*.

The key, therefore, is a robust set of a regression testing anchored on a solid *automation strategy*. This can be even better assured by creating "building blocks" in your product, with known capabilities, making it easier to isolate use cases and corner cases for these building blocks.

Crucial also is the exact replication of the production environment (what the customers run on) in the testing environment. This may be extremely difficult (how can one really simulate infinitely complex production traffic) or expensive (replicating all the layers of platform and software and connectivity) to pull off. But this investment will result in dramatically improved release confidence and outcomes. And since you will be releasing software daily, weekly, or monthly, the investment is critical to achieving operational stability.

Since SaaS is delivered over the Internet and is consumed over a web browser, the software must be certified on multiple browsers and browser versions.

SaaS software must ensure that all current use cases are handled to ensure backward compatibility to all customers. In pure SaaS, all customers are migrated to all releases immediately. There are no separate instances of software in production, and no one is "left behind." This means all customers can have access to the latest features and no customer drags on the forward-looking software-development team. This is an area where functional blocking of the software system with a known set of gates between components can simplify testing and backward compatibility testing.

SaaS Product Marketing

By its very nature, SaaS is open and accessible. This means that use cases not conceived of or explicitly identified in market studies will emerge, if one pays attention to them. A key SaaS activity in product marketing is identifying and understanding the pockets of success in the customer-install base.

The primary obsession of the product marketer should be: *How are my customers doing, and how are they using my offering?*

The product marketer has the luxury of witnessing people using the software *in real time*, because they are running the software on a shared platform. This offers the product marketer a treasure of crucial information to inspect and to learn from, with the goal of increasing value and replicating success.

This offers a real competitive advantage that one SaaS business can have over another SaaS business (let alone a competing non-SaaS business)—real-time, detailed data about all aspects of the business and the use of its products.

The product marketer should fully understand which customers are profitable and which are not. Consequently, she should set up focused product-marketing campaigns to seek more of the successful customers and provide guidance to the sales team about what kinds of deals to avoid.

Such insight from the product marketer will generate and sustain a highly virtuous cycle. The characteristics of a virtuous customer-vendor relationship tie back to the SaaS promise:

1. **The customer is happy**: That is, the product consistently solves their problems at a cost to them that they can afford without the need to own the service.

2. **The vendor is happy**: That is, the SaaS vendor is making money with this customer because:

   a. they don't need to mangle their product to fit the customer's needs (so the product and the engineering teams are happy)
   b. the customer is not coming back with issues and consuming the vendor's customer-care cycles.

True business expansion comes from driving out any inconsistencies in this relationship. The SaaS promise is hopeful but subject to gaps in (a) understanding and insight and (b) feature needs and road map velocity.

Ideally, SaaS product marketing drives

- marketing people to document success stories and educate the sales team;
- marketing people to determine how to position similar use cases in appropriate verticals with proven ROI studies for each segment;
- salespeople to close repeatable sales cycles based on marketing-driven leads tied to use cases;
- product-management teams to identify common feature gaps and road-map velocity items to inform priorities for upcoming releases with the design to *get and keep* new customers;

- the executive team to see a rational flow of activity and effort flowing among marketing leads, deals closed, successful deployments, and high retention.

When such a virtuous cycle and balance are established, the company can then move on to the next level of efficiency management: optimizing the processes and the role differentiations and fine-tuning the company and the product positioning. The result is that a clear, strong, and sustainable brand emerges—a brand backed by concrete success in the market rather than sloganeering around "the cloud" or "the solution." In major market expansions, winners buy from winners, and success breeds success.

SaaS Product Management

Product road-mapping in SaaS is a continuing balancing act between gaining new business, growing current business, and retaining current business.

In SaaS, a product road map = new features + bug fixes + feature enhancements:

- **New features:** (1) Enable *immediate revenue* from the install base, for those customers in the base who want to turn the feature on, and (2) make possible sales cycles that would be dead in the water without those features.

- **Feature enhancements:** (1) Increase retention, as customers see that they are getting more value at no additional cost, and (2) enable market expansion as the sales and marketing teams have a broader base of success to leverage in new cycles.

- **Bug fixes**: (1) Mitigate churn and (2) enable the sales team to begin leveraging customers who, having seen a problem that they had to live with resolved, are now more open to engage in new opportunity conversations.

Since SaaS is a product-centric (as opposed to a sales-centric, service-centric, or engineering-centric) business model, it is crucial that your product team is *the final arbiter on product development priorities.*

The product people—not the engineers—are the ones who know the customer base and the target market.

The product people are the ones who know what is good for the business, because they know what is good for the end user and what the market wants.

The biggest blunder that a SaaS company can commit is to let its engineering organization make product-level decisions. It is not that engineering is not *critical* to SaaS success. But engineering is not a market- or customer-facing discipline.

In other chapters, we charge Operations and Engineering with critical responsibilities of high uptime, scalability, performance, and security, which are foundational building blocks. The engineering and operations teams should have a say in

- *who* will build it,
- *where* we will build it,
- *how* we will build it, and
- *when* we will build it with quality **but not**
- *what* we will build and
- *why* we will build it!

The last two are reserved for the product and offer managers whose lives (combined with the sales and marketing team) depend upon getting these questions right.

Product determines the right thing to build, and engineering determines the right way to build right.

At best, engineering input to such decisions is often based on information that may not align with the company's growth strategy; may not be based on reality in the field or the competitive landscape;

or worse—and this happens quite often—are based on what the engineers are comfortable with or what they can best deliver or know how to deliver.

Such behavior usually leads to building the wrong product or pursuing the wrong priorities and can quickly erode the morale of the product team and lead to talent flight—talent that is highly difficult to replace.

In SaaS, an organization that has a weak product team will be dismantled by a competitor that knows (a) what the market wants and (b) how to empower its product people to deliver to that market.

SaaS Marketing

SaaS is an online offering. By definition, its customers are online: they are the *user* buyer: the buyer is actually the one who will use the service. They are not likely to be at trade-show events. They are too busy. They have real production problems in the form of sales, marketing, operations, engineering, human resources, or IT. They will be surfing the web and searching for proven solutions that solve the problem that drove them to the web.

SaaS marketing is as accessible through a simple web browser as the product. The software service that is offered lives in the same cyber location where the service is marketed and described. One doesn't go to one place to glean material about the product and to another to access the product. One goes to the very same place: the website.

Therefore, the web is where SaaS marketing begins: search engines, web content, blogs, social media, web forms, webinars, chat, e-mail, and even toll free numbers on websites—all combine, collectively pushing for that one call to action: the prospect filling out a web form, sending out an e-mail, or picking up the phone and calling. Over time, the vast web of interconnected links, success stories, referrals, and SEM and SEO activity make the website one of the most valuable assets of the SaaS business. It is the point that brings problems and identities to life.

Moreover, given the basic fact that good customers will be interacting with the service daily, and often several times a day, the opportunity is real to continually message that Customer base and to expose customers to news about Product features, customers, success stories, and promotions. Compare this continuing marketing to that, say, of the pure software vendor: having installed the software, the customer usually does not go back to the vendor's website, unless they have an issue—at which point, they are not likely to be receptive to any up-selling messaging. SaaS businesses touch their current customers with brand impressions *every day*. And one key word on the website, if placed properly, can unlock millions of dollars of cross-sell and up-sell activity.

SELLING SAAS

The natural sales opportunity in SaaS lies in the midmarket. Or, perhaps more accurately, the opportunity lies naturally with those organizations that are short both on time and on up-front money. Though many great SaaS businesses are now serving the large enterprise, this is a difficult place to drive massive initial adoption unless you have a robust starting point of initial customers.

Regardless of size of business, however, the SaaS customer is inevitably in a hurry to be up and running and to achieve time to value. The customer does not want to invest a lot of money up front to gain access to the services they are buying and not use them.

Whether the customer is a small- or medium-sized business, or a department or a unit within a larger organization, speed and reliability are crucial.

Often, such organizations may have an inadequate solution or have no solution at all to begin with.

Selling to people in a hurry requires responsiveness by the sales force: the buyer who just filled out your form is probably engaged in real-time shopping.

Indeed, *time kills SaaS leads faster than anything else.*

You are probably not the only vendor form that the potential buyer has just filled, and you are not the last one: they are probably filling out another form (that of your competitor) while you are reading the one they filled out for you.

Hence the crucial importance of *connecting while the lead is hot.*

That is why missing an incoming sales call from a fresh lead is the sales equivalent of the platform having an outage.

But perhaps the most frightening part of SaaS is the chicken-and-egg phenomenon that stalls momentum in every new market.

The first customer doesn't want to go first. The first financial application doesn't want to go first. The first $50K customer doesn't want to go first. And the same with the first $1M customer and $10MM customer.

Every new frontier is a battle for credibility on the triple test of security, reliability, and references. Have you solved this problem before? Can I talk to them? How did it go?

Every customer must be overserviced to

1. stay,
2. provide feedback necessary to improve the product,
3. be a reference, and
4. grow.

All these are the most unnatural acts for most sales team members.

Contrary to what one may think, selling in SaaS is not like protecting a maintenance stream in an enterprise software business.

It is a whole new class of service, where the service victory of one day leads to a sales victory the next and where a cross-sell opportunity can mean life or death on churn metrics. A new feature may be more important to a customer than any financial negotiation as to why they would stay.

Thus, the two fundamental metrics in SaaS are CRR and Churn.

CRR stands for *committed recurring revenue (either monthly CMRR or annual CARR).*

Churn refers to the customer or the usage attrition from the CMRR base.

The business of sales in SaaS is to increase the CMRR base and to minimize the churn. This means to close new logos, close the right customers, retain the base, and add to the base of the CMRR.

To that goal, the SaaS sales team is divided into two subteams: hunters and farmers.

Hunters exist to bring new logos into the customer base—i.e., *new blood.*

Farmers exist to secure the customer base—i.e., secure the CMRR base. And the best way to secure that customer base is to continually provide additional value, service, and a listening ear to that base: that is, to continually serve that base and sell into that base.

The Circle of SaaS

The problem with *the sales learning curve* and climbing it is tied to *the circle of SaaS*: Operations drives uptime, which drives retention; Engineering drives features, which become a product; product drives marketing leads and lead conversion rates, which drive sales; sales drive customers, which become references and, in turn, drive product needs and further drive uptime requirements. And around the SaaS circle goes.

Like all circles, the SaaS circle has no beginning and no end. The business starts with a few fortunate wins and then evolves through the art of jumping in the middle and creating expansion value for each and every new customer, and thus *organically* grow the SaaS circle.

As a SaaS business, a key benefit that enables this circle to begin is that your customers are essentially online and you can generate leads from scratch with modest marketing dollars.

The Sales Learning Curve

Here are a few tips on climbing the sales learning curve:

1. **Colocate the sales team**: Crucial to the success of the SaaS Sales team is the colocation of the team with the rest of the organization. Such colocation is crucial because SaaS is *a way of living* that needs to be inculcated into the sales force: the speed of action, the familiarity with the product, and the constant learning, are not possible when the sales agent lives away from the mother ship. Know this: *standalone SaaS sales teams will fail*. In SaaS, a single building with all the critical functions, from sales and marketing to operations and engineering, drives a common mind-set to *live to serve the customers*. The colocation of sales agents is possible given that most of the leads are web-generated and, hence, can be handled from anywhere (to engage, the sales agent does not need to live where the prospect lives) and the service will be delivered remotely—the very nature of SaaS. And given that technology now makes possible truly rich interactions

(web-casting, chatting), a sales cycle can go very far without the salesperson meeting the customer face-to-face. SaaS salespeople are comfortable meeting, presenting, fact-finding, demoing, *and* closing online.

2. **Measure your travel cost, but go if needed**: Nonetheless, for the larger deals (large in the eyes the customer), a face-to-face, eye-to-eye meeting, or several such meetings, will be needed before fully closing the deal. Buying SaaS requires a great deal of *trust*, and such trust often needs the full human touch to be meaningfully established. Some $50K deals require it, and some $500K don't. Stall without it. A competent SaaS sales executive knows where to go and when to go. But do make sure you are measuring this cost against sales results. But don't keep your sales teams inside if they need to go to advance critical sales cycles.

3. **Learn your lessons**: Create a format for learning from every success and every failure: closed-deal format where each lesson is learned. *Such learning is true, durable, and hard to replicate capital.* It is as real a competitive advantage as any technology.

4. **Measure marketing**: Make sure each expenditure in SEM/SEO, trade show, webinar, and analyst relationship is measured. If there is no clear ROI over twelve to eighteen months, *kill it*. When you find something that works, *double down or triple down*.

5. **Hire only two to three salespeople, and sit with them in the sales bull pen.** Do not sit in your office. If you don't have $1MM in CMRR, you are still learning. Get out there, and learn and contribute to the solution and the learning.

6. **Create epicenters**: Build focused case studies that show how your solution solves a specific problem. If you have already solved that problem for a deployed, happy customer, document it. Write white papers, data sheets, and record videos showing the solution to this problem. Once you have your first customers, get them to do a testimonial on their solution. Each epicenter becomes central to every sales pitch and a theme for a microsite, trade show, webinar, or e-mail campaign. As a sales tool, a solid epicenter contains at minimum

   • A short PowerPoint presentation outlining a specific problem, a specific solution, key differentiators, and attributes that are your unique claims.
   • A demo that supports the solution and quickly proves the claims. When you demo, you win in SaaS because you are proving your claims. Your buyer doesn't have to decide whether to believe your claims but whether they need what your claims provide.
   • Backup materials such as data sheets if the business is technical, white papers, case studies, or other relevant leave-behinds that support the resonant claims.

7. **Measure activity**: Measure leads, calls, e-mails, opportunities, phone calls, and sales activities. You will gain a competitive advantage if you shape your organization to be disciplined enough to routinely deliver such measurement. You need to program the process for success in order to scale. If the sales rep isn't getting a first sale—no matter how small—in the first ninety days, say good-bye to them. They are either not ready for SaaS, or your *management* is not ready for SaaS.

8. **Understand your SEM and SEO**: Determine which SEM and SEO terms are actually driving success. Make changes incrementally, or you will not know which are working. Hire *outsiders* to do your SEM/SEO work as they are more likely to stay up with the latest technology and techniques.

SaaS Professional Services

It is often said that in the "perfect" SaaS company, the professional-services group would not exist. The proposition is almost by definition self-defeating, given that in this definition of "perfection," the SaaS offering would become a "cloud island," when at the very essence of the cloud ecosystem is the ability between clouds to interact with one another. Such a SaaS offering would be the opposite of perfect: it would be fundamentally flawed.

The professional services (PS) organization in SaaS should be viewed primarily as an enabler of committed monthly recurring revenue—and not as a critical revenue stream in its own right. If PS is not focused on (a) enabling time to value, (b) delivering recurring revenue, and (c) driving satisfied customers, then there is a disconnect between the various SaaS business stakeholders.

The head of PS must view their mission as one of maximizing total revenue and attaining an overall profit margin (not a PS margin). The primary metrics should be *how to turn out deployments quickly, reliably, and with an reliability target equal to that of the core platform.*

A SaaS PS team should strive to make a customer as happy on the day after the initial cutover as they were the moment they signed the purchase order. Think about how confident a business manager must be on the day of signature. Why should they not feel the same on the day of live operation—and beyond? The primary balancing act should be between speed and quality—not between cost and revenue. Of course, financial prudence is important. But a break-even PS business with happy recurring revenue customers beats any amount of PS margin that delays recurring revenue from kicking in. Further, PS gross profits should not be taken at the expense of delaying the deployment of a project or the uptime of that customer upon deployment. In the end, what really matters are recurring revenue and uptime.

An important challenge that a professional services organization must deal with in a SaaS business is the disruption caused by complex deployments. The ideal situation would be that the distribution of complexity across deployments is even—all customer deployments are equally complex. This is desirable because it enables

1. linear growth of the professional services team, enabling thus,

2. the consistent hiring of quality staff—since the hiring is happening deliberately, proactively, and continually and over an extended period (rather than in fits and *en masse*, as would happen in the case of a new disproportionally large deployment), and

3. the minimizing of idle work cycles.

However, given that complex projects will inevitably fall into the path of the SaaS professional services organization, an overflow strategy is core to ensuring the sustainable integrity of the professional-services group. Integration partners, running the gamut from highly skilled, reliable individual freelancers, to large integration organizations, need to be part of the professional-services ecosystem, with a well-defined process for engaging, maintaining, and broadening that ecosystem. Such a function—managing integration partners—needs to be fully differentiated and assigned to an owner, whose role is to ensure that the PS organization will be ready to take on complex projects with minimal internal disruption to the PS organization. It is dangerous to become PS-constrained in SaaS and equally problematic to have a large portion of the team consumed in a small number of projects. Partners can help manage this feast-and-famine expansion.

SaaS Customer Care

Given the nature of SaaS—one software for all on one platform for all—the care organization experiences intense spikes of activities upon service disruptions.

The successful care organization is one that knows how to handle crises: its leaders need to be unflappable and able to retain both their calm and their ability to think when a crisis hits, whether the problems pertains to an unexpected use case in the system, a major system problem, or an unexpected spike in demand.

In a successful SaaS care organization, all members of that organization are intimately familiar with the product. They know the product more than anyone else in the organization, including the product managers. They are familiar not only with all its features, and across all product lines that are supported, but also with its flaws and how it is actually used across customers in the field. Most crucially, they are familiar with the product's primary use cases.

The successful SaaS care organization doesn't stop when the customer trouble case is closed. The team has a well-defined process for continually enhancing the knowledge base to better serve incoming queries for help. Such a knowledge base should be intrinsic to the product and continuously updated and augmented and should be available, searchable, and editable online. Help should be an intrinsic product feature, and care teams should be at the front line of updating the knowledge base.

As a result of the depth and breadth of their expertise, the SaaS care organization becomes a powerfully effective incubator of future successful members of other organizations in the business. The successful care professional is a person who can communicate effectively, knows the product inside out, knows how to troubleshoot it, knows how to demo it, understands use cases and market problems intimately, and is able to handle the pressures of a crisis. Most importantly, the SaaS care professional understands the centrality of *Time* in SaaS business: the need to respond quickly makes all the difference in the world. A professional equipped with such skills can comfortably transition into Product, Operations, Quality Assurance, Account Management, Sales Engineering, and Sales. Staff your care organization with smart, ambitious, technically capable, and friendly people, and you will be creating a feeder pool for more than a dozen functions in your business.

SaaS Partnerships

By "partnerships," we mean an alliance between several businesses with the purpose of leveraging natural synergies that will lead to profitable revenue for all sides of the partnership. A successful partnership is a two-way street where both partners *acknowledge each other as equal participants* in a common enterprise. The best partnerships go *strength to strength* and are not put in place solely to minimize a weakness of one party or maximize the interests of the other.

Successful partnerships place relatively equal burden on all sides and reap relatively equal benefits to all sides. A partnership where one partner is bearing the brunt of an integration or who spends real sales and marketing dollars or who assumes support for a joint offering, with no reciprocal contribution from the other partner, is not a healthy partnership. A partnership where one partner is reaping real revenue from the relationship, while the other partner is not, is doomed to failure.

In SaaS, partnerships are natural to seek but hard to execute. Rich offerings are available in some form of a cloud or another, with the temptation of expanding value by establishing a link between clouds following naturally.

However, what must be kept in mind are the following:

1. If you seek a cloud partner, ensure first and foremost that they take their uptime as seriously as you do yours.

2. Ensure that they have a happy, growing customer base that you can build on and add to your base. A partnership should never be a lifeline or a crutch. You have precious little time to manage partnerships, and they should be selected carefully and gain extreme focus.

A good test of how much you value a partnership is whether you are willing to dedicate at least one *full-time* person or a team to manage this relationship. If you are, then proceed. If you are not, then don't waste your time and your partner's time.

Partnerships can take many forms, but here are the primary types of partnerships forged during the development of the SaaS business and a key lesson for each type:

- **Professional services:** The goal for these partnerships is to augment professional services capacity. In reality, you will need to have a steady flow to make such partnerships work. Pick one or two partners, and make sure you always have at least two full-time resources fully occupied with each partner in order to keep them liquid in the relationship. Start-stop arrangements. Don't worry about the profitability of resold PS. Remember, as a SaaS business, your primary mission is to get customers live and happy quickly, not to pad professional services margins.
- **Technology partnerships:** These are formed to create adjacent capabilities or acquire core components for your solution. When building a SaaS platform, it is often inevitable that some critical component will be costly. A SaaS leader should devise a strategy to partner closely with key element providers in the supply chain to develop long-run incremental

cost structures that minimize gross margin drag. One such method is to purchase large quantities in bulk with a final bulk quantity that gives a platform site license to the firm with a smaller escalator on the maintenance fee. This allows your vendors to make higher margin money from you up front, but then to reduce their drag on your business as you expand. This ensures you will not likely engineer them out of your solution as you become broadly successful. Such rewards may take many years and orders of magnitude growth to achieve, but they can enable significant gross-margin expansion as the firm succeeds.

- **Channel partner:** Such partnerships are designed to drive revenue. In the end, the only way they will accomplish this is if they have (a) a strong brand that you don't have; (b) a market reach you don't have (e.g., a country); (c) a value add that uniquely positions the combined offering. Achieving successful channel partnerships in SaaS is very difficult, as you are still figuring out your products, how to market and sell them, thus making it impossible to teach someone else how to succeed. It is better to wait until you have a critical channel issue you cannot solve on your own before engaging in channel-partner activities.

Legal SaaS

Legal can become an extremely weighty anchor for a SaaS business. Agility and responsiveness are at the heart of what makes a SaaS business successful. A legal department that does not move at the speed of SaaS needs to be replaced with one that does.

In the early days, use a standard form and seek external contract counsel only for big deals. As a phase 2, upgrade to a SaaS contracts manager. Only in phase 3 should you hire a full-time contract attorney.

It is important to note that the legal department is as intrusive and obstructive as the opportunity given to it to be so. A contract that has no redlines returned from a customer will not offer an opportunity to intrude or obstruct. Therefore, key to enabling Legal to move at the speed of SaaS is to pursue deals that require minimal change to the standard contract and to drive sales processes that invite little change. (When was the last time you redlined the clickwrap on an Apple ios app you downloaded?)

Certain additional processes and procedures can be set up to keep legal from becoming an obstacle. These articles of confederation are a good start:

1) **Lead with uptime**: Put your 99.999 percent uptime SLA online, and live up to it. Your life depends upon it. While you are at it, make it 100 percent. Take this issue off the table.

2) **Create a balanced boilerplate, and put it online**: Most of your midmarket customers will respect a balanced draft and click-wrap accept with no changes.

3) **Make ordering easy:** Use an electronic signature service (such as *Docusign*) to enable purchase orders, change orders, new CMMR commitments, and professional services SOWs to be signed via e-mail. Make all orders refer back to the online MSA and SLA.

4) **When negotiations are required, be sure they are for the entire corporation**: A broad multiyear MSA with "Walmart" is invaluable even if it takes nine months to negotiate.

5) **Have backup language**: If your limitation of liability standard is equal to fees paid but for breach of confidentiality you are willing to budge, have that language prewritten and preapproved by your Legal for deals over some set threshold.

6) **Be up-front on security**: Establish clearly your security framework, document both sides of responsibility, and live up to them.

7) **Don't ask for redlines:** Many sales reps will send the contract "out for redlines." Don't permit this. Send purchase orders with clickable links to online standard MSAs attached. Business users will appreciate this and choose speed if they have real business problems.

SaaS Finance

In SaaS, *cash is king*!

Keeping a very close eye on the numbers—cost, revenue, bookings, pipeline—is a vital finance function. It takes quite a bit of funding to deploy a SaaS service, engineer a solution, learn how to reduce *churn, climb the sales learning curve*, the *uptime learning curve*, and uncovering the *cross-sell moments*. Once there, climb faster because you have now made a market and others will quickly follow. But always *watch your cash burn rate*. Cash is essential for the first two- to three-year business-proving phase.

Finance is the only neutral organization within the business that can ensure that the financial health of the business is *constantly* being monitored. But turn your finance leader into a finance operations leader, helping you drive all the business metrics. A P and L is useless if you are out of money. And nothing will predict losses faster than increasing uptime and churn.

In SaaS, *time and timing are of the essence*. Rapid growth can be just as devastating as stunted or no growth. Letting customers slip on their payments can be hugely detrimental as revenue targets may be missed or key strategic numbers not met.

If you are the CEO or CFO, get your bank statement e-mailed to you every morning. Check it every day right after you check your usage, website hits, and new customers in trial and closed that day.

Is the cash OK? Is the usage OK? Are collections OK? Well, then great—the day is off to a SaaSy start! Now back to harassing the sales reps.

SaaS Support Systems

Your business is SaaSy: you need to eat SaaS systems for breakfast, lunch, and dinner.

Your Billing, Support, CRM, HR, and *Wiki* all had better be in the cloud.

You will see things in these systems you can leverage. You will find partners.

You will see connections.

Chances are that, any of the systems that you are using could probably use your system in return.

At a minimum, you should be using SaaS CRM, ERP, HR, marketing automation, and product-tracking systems.

Table Stakes Metrics

In order of importance, below are the critical SaaS metrics. You *cannot* advance to the next metric until you *own* the previous metrics. And you should *not* spend time on the advanced metrics until the table stakes are met.

This is where you start. Many of these metrics are the seed of the metrics you will manage in the more mature SaaS business—but does *churn* really matter when you have five customers and you lost two? Yes! Forty percent churn is terrible. What matters is *understanding why you lost* that customer and whether you can fix *your business* to prevent a similar loss in the future. It also enables you to understand enough to potentially commence a win-back campaign.

1. **Cash**: Can you make payroll next month?

2. **Uptime:** There is no point closing your next customer deal if you are going to go down tomorrow. *Fix this first*, and put processes in place to *keep it fixed.*

3. **New leads generated:** Hopefully, these are online web forms but can also be lists you are cold-calling based on your target market.

4. **New trials/pilots started:** If possible, this happens automatically through an online portal. You need to have

robust procedures to touch them on day 1, day 7, day 15, and day 30, before the trial period ends.

5. **New opportunities created:** These are leads that pass the Ideal customer criteria and have the potential to benefit from the solution.

6. **New customers:** A win is a win. No matter how small or how big, celebrate all your wins. Have a big bell, and ring it joyfully when you gain a new customer. In SaaS, with the proper love and care, a $1,000/month win can eventually lead to a profitable $1MM revenue stream.

7. **Customer tickets this month:** Your entire management team should see every ticket from every customer. And your product managers must be as keen on understanding these issues as your support, operations, and engineering teams are in resolving them in real time. Repeat tickets should be treated like repeat infractions—*infractions by your business against your customers.*

8. **Customers who quit today:** You need to learn everything you can about these. If it was business failure, move on—welcome to the world of early SaaS. If it was uptime, *get back to item 2.* If it was missing features, try to get them back with a commitment for completion of the features—but only if the features are already on your road map.

9. **Stories completed:** You should plan for, understand, and celebrate each new "story" or use case solved by your agile product-development team. Each one may ultimately save, create, or enable a new, future customer some day. Make your engineers part of the metrics story.

10. **Customers live today:** Make sure you differentiate between closing a deal and a customer *using* the service. *If they don't use, you will lose.* That is, if they are paying you without getting any benefit, they will naturally cancel their contract next time it is up for approval.

11. **Usage:** Determine some method for measuring usage—whether it is logins, processes, transactions executed, or time in the system. If your system is gaining, losing, or maintaining momentum, you need to know. Watch this on a customer-specific basis, and put your farmers to work diagnosing and solving usage slumps and taking advantage of usage spikes and acceleration.

HIRING SAASY PEOPLE

Finding and hiring great people in SaaS is harder than finding and hiring great people to build and sell traditional software.

SaaS people need to think with agility, quality, and scalability in mind—*and* they need to have a service mentality. Software as a service involves both of these "s" words.

Experience in SaaS is far more important than experience in a vertical of expertise.

If you find salespeople who have successfully sold SaaS for financial planning, hire them. Don't debate whether you should hire someone who is an expert salesman in your vertical (say customer-care solutions) but has never sold SaaS. The SaaS and service orientation will better serve your quest for talent in the long run.

Experience in service is more important than experience in software or in technology.

If you find a great customer-care person who fielded issues for a utility company, hire them before you consider hiring someone who did care for a pure software company, even if the company delivered something in your vertical.

Look for action-oriented people who also believe in process and in acting systematically.

You don't want pure firefighters, and you don't want pure bureaucrats. You need smart business athletes who are constantly learning about how to deliver success and how to replicate that success across the organization.

Such people are rare, so always be on the lookout for them. Keep asking around for great people. Ask your prospects and your customers: Who has impressed them in their sales skills, customer success skills, UI skills? Ask your vendors and your partners. They get called and are constantly being sold and are consuming products and services, and if you ask, they may point you to people they think are exceptional.

EVOLVING METRICS

As you begin to make progress on the top 10, you can begin migrating to the more advanced SaaS metrics.

1. **Uptime by product**
2. **CMRR (committed monthly recurring revenue)**
3. **Churn percentage**, by product, by customer type, age of customer, and reason for churn
4. **Marketing ROI by program** (trade show, SEM/SEO)
5. **Customer lifetime value** (CLV)
6. **Customer acquisition cost** (CaC)
7. **CaC payback ratio**
8. **Cash flow**
9. **CMRR pipeline**
10. **Orders this month**: CMRR, professional services, new versus existing
11. **New logos this month**
12. **Your P and L**
13. **Customer report rate by product**
14. **Mean time to resolve customer-issue report**
15. **Customer repeat-trouble report rate**
16. **PS cycle time**
17. **Number of software releases per month**

THE SaaS BOTTOM LINE

1. **SaaS is a bottom line, not a top line, business.** If you are not constantly watching your bottom line and ensuring that you are not bleeding, you will soon find that you have built a Frankenstein-like organization and that you have wasted valuable time creating the illusion of success rather than the foundations of a great, successful SaaS business.

   In SaaS, there rarely are such things as "a good problem to have." As in "let's close the deal and worry about the road map implications later." Such problems are bad problems because they disrupt and mangle the SaaS machine that you are trying to build.

   And if at any time you do decide that you are not going to be profitable, be so deliberately—that is, if you want to be in the red, be in the red not because you are closing big but unprofitable deals. Do it because you are deliberately reinvesting in your business—mainly, reinvesting in your product, your marketing, your sales, and your run-time operations.

2. **The service part of SaaS doesn't mean that you turn the business into a consulting gig.** If your professional services organization is larger than your product and marketing organizations or your engineering and operations organizations, then you have a problem—a serious one.

3. **If more than 50 percent of your professional services team are working on deploying one customer at any given time, then you have a serious problem**. And that problem is not a professional services organization problem but a product, strategy, or leadership problem.

4. **SaaS is a product-marketing-centric business model.** It is not a consulting-based model or a sales-based model or an exercise in technology innovation. The business proposition is the establishment of a well-defined customer base that consumes a well-defined service product that solves a well-defined set of problems.

5. **Don't be opportunistic—be dogmatic and systematic.** Create a product that a big-enough market will find valuable. Deliver the most usable and useful product to that market that you can deliver with the money that you have. Find those customers who will love to buy your product. Find more of them. If a big whale comes along that wants you to mangle your product in exchange for their dollars, don't chase that whale. Don't be opportunistic in that way. You would be chasing the wrong kind of whale. This does not necessarily mean that you systematically turn down large, game-changing deals that accelerate where you are taking your business. But when contemplate doing so, make sure you have the support of your board, your management team, and your investors.

6. **The only whale you should be chasing is the organization that you are building.** It's a big-enough whale to keep you constantly thrilled.

7. **Your SaaS growth strategy is to close those customers who buy from you for your value.** Find more of those customers, and thoughtfully evolve your product by listening carefully to

them and adding those features and services that align with where you want to go with those customers and the market.

8. **Be willing to fire customers. It's hard, but sometimes it's the healthy and right thing to do.** You may discover that in the process, the customer will actually move to align with what it will take to turn them into, and keep them as, a profitable customer.

9. **Your board needs to think strategically and needs to understand the nature of SaaS.** They should judge whether or not the business is successful by understanding the types of customers that are being closed and served. Top line or growth rate in SaaS are not reliable measures of business health. Indeed, they can be—and often are—very misleading. Scalability is the only true measure of health in SaaS. It takes a thoughtful, deliberate, and patient board that thinks long term, and not quarter by quarter, to guide the business, heads down, in the right direction. Pick those people who truly understand SaaS to be members of your board.

10. **Educate the owners.** Make sure that whoever is financing the business understands that SaaS is about growing a healthy revenue-generating machine and not about making the sales growth chart look good at any cost.

11. **Measure individual customer profitability.** It's hard enough to measure the profitability of a business in general, but it's much harder to measure the profitability of any given customer. It requires you to keep close tabs on the marketing dollars spent to acquire the customer, the cost of the sales effort (length of cycle, who got involved in the cycle, expenses of closing the deal—trips, entertainment, etc.), the amount of time and money spent to deploy the customer, the support that

the customer is consuming once they have been deployed, the amount of money they are paying you, the discounts that you had to give them because of penalties (e.g., service disruptions), and the effort that you have expended collecting money from them. But if you somehow manage to get the business to the point where it can systematically measure the profitability of any given customer, then you have built a formidable machine that few other organizations will be able to compete against. Your organization's discipline will be one of your core business assets and differentiators.

12. It takes a strong team to pull off SaaS.

It takes a strong head of operations: someone who believes in process and who has the stomach to live under the constant challenge of keeping the service up 100 percent of the time.

It takes a strong head of product: someone who is able to say no to bad product requests from Sales (the whale chasers, especially) and the business—requests that do not align or prioritize with the product strategy.

It takes a strong COO: someone who obsesses about process and profitability and is not fooled by numbers that can lie.

It takes a strong CEO: someone who will go to the mat repeatedly to keep his team focused on building a profitable, scalable SaaS business. This CEO needs to spend his or her time educating and evangelizing to the owners and the board on how to measure the health of a SaaS business and what the team needs to keep the business on a healthy, sustainable growth path.

It takes a wise and ethical board: a board that understands that SaaS is not about making a quick buck but about making a lasting, recurring buck in due time. The board needs to understand that SaaS is about building something great. And building something great requires a clear vision, a well-defined plan, great people who understand SaaS and who execute—and patience to see the business through its growth phases.

Made in the USA
San Bernardino, CA
09 July 2016